Bibliographical S
of Supplements to 'British Bo...
on Writers and Their Work

★

GENERAL EDITOR
Geoffrey Bullough

¶ Robert Southey was born in Bristol on 12 August 1774. He died on 21 March 1843.

ROBERT SOUTHEY

Detail from a painting by SIR THOMAS LAWRENCE *in the*
National Gallery of South Africa

ROBERT SOUTHEY

by

GEOFFREY CARNALL

PUBLISHED FOR
THE BRITISH COUNCIL
AND THE NATIONAL BOOK LEAGUE
BY LONGMANS, GREEN & CO.

LONGMANS, GREEN & CO. LTD.
48 Grosvenor Street, London W.1

*Associated companies, branches and
representatives throughout the world*

First published 1964
© Geoffrey Carnall 1964

*Printed in Great Britain by
F. Mildner & Sons, London, E.C.1*

ROBERT SOUTHEY

I

ROBERT Southey saw himself as a dominating figure in the England of his day. He was the author of several major poems, and an intrepid innovator in his subjects and his metres. His literary achievement had been publicly recognised when he was made Poet Laureate—the King's own poet. As a prominent contributor to the *Quarterly Review*, he exercized a powerful influence on public life. As an historian, he was a pioneer in recording the development of the vast new nation of Brazil. In his *History of the Peninsular War*, he celebrated what seemed to him the most inspiriting event of his time—the Spaniards' general and simultaneous insurrection against the mighty military power of Napoleon's France.

Southey shared to the full in that restless energy so characteristic of the Napoleonic era. It was a time of grandiose political and philosophical systems, and was prolific in plans for treatises, histories, and epic poems. The results were often disappointing, and Southey would certainly have been disappointed at the relatively small part assigned to him in English literary history. His most memorable work is seldom even thought of as his. Few people associate 'The Story of the Three Bears' with his name. His *Life of Nelson* is still being reprinted, but it is for the great admiral's sake, not Southey's. 'The Battle of Blenheim' and 'The Inchcape Rock' have almost acquired the anonymity of folklore. If Southey is remembered as a man, it is as the ridiculous figure in Byron's 'Vision of Judgement'. He is still a stock example (partly because of his association with Wordsworth and Coleridge) of the ardent young reformer who is corrupted and turns conservative. Social historians, however, sometimes honour him as an early critic of the evils which the new factory system brought to early nineteenth-century Britain. He made a notable protest against the commercial spirit, regarding it as deeply injurious to the kindly and generous feelings of human nature. Yet his protests are no longer read as those of Carlyle and Dickens are.

He was endowed with a strong sensibility—too strong, in fact. His senses, he confessed, were perilously acute: 'impressions sink into me too deeply. . . . I fly from one thing to another, each new train of thought neutralizing, as it were, the last.' Such a method of writing would seem to guarantee a failure to achieve fully satisfactory expression. Yet his work constantly betrays the feelings which he found almost unendurable. This is particularly true of his copious and unguarded correspondence; but from nearly all his work the attentive reader will learn something of the stresses under which men lived in his time: a time of exceptionally rapid social change and insecurity.

II

Southey was born in Bristol on 12 August, 1774. He came from a family of farmers and tradespeople, his own father being a linen-draper. Much of his childhood was spent under the capricious care of a maiden aunt with some pretensions to gentility, Miss Tyler. She utterly dominated his mother: 'never', Southey wrote later, 'did I know one person so entirely subjected by another.' This early experience of domestic despotism probably helped to create the rather bleak view of life that casts a shadow over nearly all his writings. He was a sensitive child, and his family enjoyed making him cry by forcing him to listen to sad songs and dismal stories. He reacted against this overmastering sensibility by developing military ambitions. At the age of nine, he read Shakespeare's history plays, concluded that England was now once again on the brink of civil war, and made up his mind to take a leading part in the conflict. In order to enlist followers, he set up as an interpreter of dreams, referring his schoolfellows' dreams to the coming great civil wars and the appearance of a very great man—meaning himself.

The stratagem was ingenious, but apparently did not work. His literary ambitions developed later, and were much more successful. Being an enthusiastic admirer of Spenser's 'Faerie Queene', he decided to finish the poem. Before he was fifteen, he had sketched a plan based on every hint he could gather from the six books which Spenser himself had completed. Southey actually wrote three cantos of this projected continuation. Nothing, he said, ever gave him so much delight as the dream of what he intended to do in it.

The predominant impulse in this and other early projects seems to have been one of constructing a world of his own, in which the menacing forces outside him could be contended with on terms more advantageous than everyday life often allowed. The appeal of the remote and exotic is specially apparent in the plan he formed to illustrate various national mythologies, each with its own heroic poem. His later epics were in part a fulfilment of this scheme.

Southey was fifteen when the French Revolution began, and he soon became a passionate sympathizer with the revolutionary cause. He was expelled from Westminster School for writing an attack on flogging (he proved it to be an invention of the Devil). Later, at Balliol College, Oxford, he felt himself increasingly at odds with the course of life arranged for him. His uncle, the Rev. Herbert Hill, who was Chaplain to the British Factory at Lisbon, wanted his nephew to become a clergyman. But Southey had little relish for this. Modern geology and Gibbon's history had undermined his belief in the Bible. As a democrat he objected to a system which gave bishops incomes of £10,000 a year. As an enthusiastic reader of Goethe's *Werther* he was inclined to question the ethical doctrines of Christianity. It is true that he learned to reject the sensibility of *Werther* for the fortitude and self-control of stoicism as

interpreted by Epictetus. But this was not enough to overcome his distaste for the Church. He could see only one way
out. He must emigrate.

The idea of emigration took a firm shape in 1794, when
he met Samuel Taylor Coleridge, then an undergraduate at
Cambridge. Between them they evolved a plan for a
settlement in America (first Kentucky, and later Pennsylvania), to be run on egalitarian, 'pantisocratic' principles.
Although the plan came to nothing, for a time it had an
intoxicating effect on both men. They lived in Bristol, and
took a prominent part in radical agitation there. They gave
lectures, and wrote propagandist pieces. The one which
became most famous in the end was Southey's poetic play
about Wat Tyler. This leader of the Peasants' Revolt in the
fourteenth century had become a type of the spirit of radical
reform. Southey affected to regard him as an ancestor: was
not his genteel aunt a Miss Tyler? Inspired by this personal
association, he denounced the aristocrats with uninhibited
enjoyment:

> Be he villain, be he fool,
> Still to hold despotic rule,
> Trampling on his slaves with scorn!
> This is to be nobly born.

As the prospect of emigration receded, however, his
revolutionary ardour cooled. It no longer seemed so difficult
to make a living in England. A school-friend, Charles Wynn,
gave him an annuity, and the Bristol bookseller Joseph Cottle,
who later published the *Lyrical Ballads* of Wordsworth and
Coleridge, issued a handsome edition of Southey's first epic
poem, 'Joan of Arc'. This soon gained him a considerable
literary reputation. After some desultory efforts to study law,
he gradually settled into the life of a professional man of
letters: a vocation which was confirmed when in 1803 he
went to live at Greta Hall in Keswick, in the Lake District
of the north of England. Coleridge was already staying
there. He had married Sarah Fricker, a sister of Southey's

wife Edith; and the two families formed the nucleus of a large household, of which Southey's letters give a pleasant picture.

Before this final settlement in Keswick, he spent two considerable periods with his uncle in Portugal. It was here that he developed his interest in Portuguese and Spanish history and literature, a subject on which he became the leading English authority. His first impressions of the country, indeed, were unfavourable. He found the squalid poverty repulsive, and had little good to say for the Roman Catholic Church. Still, he preferred Catholicism to the Calvinistic forms of protestantism which he knew in England, because it did more to kindle and satisfy the feelings and the imagination:

Bad indeed must the sinner be who will not be burnt white at last! Every prayer at a crucifix helps him—and a Mass on purpose is a fine *shove* towards Paradise. It is a superstition of hope.

The power lent by Catholic belief, in alliance with the strong national feelings of the people, enabled the Spaniards to resist the French after the invasion of 1808. Southey heard country people talk of their old heroes, and 'witnessed the passionate transfiguration which a Spaniard underwent when recurring from the remembrance of those times to his own'. In the chivalric literature of Spain, much of which Southey translated into English, it was possible to find an antidote to the sense of weakness which he found so difficult to tolerate. As the Cid smote down his enemies, so Southey delighted to trample on his.

He never found any difficulty in provoking opposition. 'Joan of Arc' is a calculatedly controversial poem: English readers were not used to seeing their heroic King Henry V consigned to hell. His shorter poems and ballads, like Wordsworth's, are particularly concerned with the common people and their sufferings. In his 'Botany Bay Eclogues' he enters sympathetically into the condition of convicts who had been transported to Australia. He exploits popular traditions, and deliberately avoids sophistication. As the Scots critic Francis Jeffrey remarked, the new sect of poets had a 'perverted taste for simplicity' and a 'splenetic and idle discontent with the institutions of society'. Southey's most scoffed-at poems were his experiments in metres borrowed from Greek and Latin poetry. The trouble was that he wrote about subjects his readers found ludicrously unclassical —beggars and screaming babies.

Thus, although Southey was no longer the young revolutionary of 1794, he was still seen by the public as an unorthodox poet, hostile to the established order of things. After 1810, however, he acquired a very different reputation. He became a warm partisan of public order, an outspoken Tory. His views changed in the first instance because of political controversies over the Peninsular War. When the Spaniards rose against the French in 1808, the news was enthusiastically welcomed in Britain, eager for new allies in the long and exhausting war with France. Southey's joy was unbounded. All that the chivalry of Spain had meant to his imagination seemed now to be realized in political action. As the Spanish campaign dragged on, however, and Napoleon continued to dominate Europe, a mood of war-weariness began to increase in Britain. The opposition parties took a gloomy view of the war in Spain, and Southey came to feel that only the conservative government of Spencer Perceval could be relied on to back the Spaniards. Hence Wat Tyler's apologist was converted to support for the unreformed British Constitution, which may have kept power in the hands of a few rich men, but did at least ensure a strong administration. Any reform which gave more influence to the middle and lower classes would be intolerable.

It was not only the war that made Southey conservative. He was also alarmed at the increasingly turbulent state of British politics. The industrial system had shattered traditional social loyalties. It had created a society which was callous and irresponsible. He was appalled by the conditions of life in towns like Birmingham and Manchester, and especially by the employment of children in factories. 'I thought', he wrote in his *Letters from England*, 'that if Dante had peopled one of his hells with children, here was a scene worthy to have supplied him with new images of torment.' Prosperity was founded on the brutalization of the great mass of the people. As he put it once in the *Quarterly Review*, the modern industrial system

carries in itself the sure cause of its own terrible destruction. That physical force which it has brought together as an instrument of lucration —a part of its machinery—will one day explode under high pressure.

There would be a terrible war of the poor against the rich. With serious riots in London in 1810, the 'Luddite' machine-breaking in some factory areas in 1812, and above all, in the same year, the assassination of the Prime Minister, Spencer Perceval, it looked as though violent revolution were an immediate danger. Southey's own radicalism had been violent, and he detected the same mood in the reform movement as a whole. Many well-disposed friends of order were not, he felt, sufficiently disturbed by the trend of events. From his retreat in Keswick Southey sought to sound the alarm, and to point out the means of reforming society so that the pressures making for revolution could be contained and removed.

From its first number in 1809, he had been a leading contributor to the *Quarterly Review*, a journal closely associated with Perceval's administration. It was here that he expounded his views on the measures necessary to save the country. Strong government was the first need: trouble-makers should be transported to Australia, where they would have less scope for mischief. But his articles were not mere pleas for repression. He recognized that social inequality like that found in England was utterly wrong. He sympathized with the pioneering socialist plans of Robert Owen,

seeing in them a practical application of the ideals of panti-
socracy, to which he still felt a strong attachment. He even
commended the revolutionary society of 'Spencean philan-
thropists', insofar as they aimed at building experimental
socialist communities. His main interest, however, was in
universal education (on sound and law-abiding principles),
and in assisted emigration.

Southey's services to public order and social reform were
not confined to journalism. In 1813 he agreed to accept the
office of Poet Laureate. The duties of this office consisted
mainly in supplying poems for royal weddings and other
court occasions, and Southey's immediate predecessor had
been a poet of very modest talents, Henry James Pye. For a
reputable man of letters it required much boldness to under-
take the work at all. But Southey had conceived the idea of
using his laureate poems to strengthen the spirit of order and
true patriotism. The Poet Laureate was to give utterance to
the soul of the nation. He wrote irregular odes to keep up
the people's will to win the war, to commend schemes of
welfare, and to deplore insane faction, rabid treason, and
erring zeal. When the Princess Charlotte married, he wrote
a 'Lay of the Laureate' in which her royal duties were
clearly detailed, and her latter end plainly set before her:

> Is this the Nuptial Song? with brow severe
>   Perchance the votaries of the world will say:
> Are these fit strains for Royal ears to hear?
>   What man is he who thus assorts his lay,
> And dares pronounce with inauspicious breath,
> In Hymeneal verse, the name of Death?

A year later the Princess was indeed dead—and Southey
wrote a decorous Funeral Song. His most ambitious, and
most disastrous, laureate poem was inspired by the death (in
1820) of George III. 'A Vision of Judgement' relates how the
poet witnesses the king's triumphant entry into heaven—a
ceremony which the powers of darkness would like to
prevent, but cannot. George, rejuvenated and restored to

sanity, is greeted by his royal ancestors, and by great
Englishmen of the past. Southey is particularly delighted to
catch a glimpse of Spenser, whose poetry caught him up into
a world of romance which made the real world 'weary, and
stale, and flat'. Indeed, the Poet Laureate was so eager to
join the departed worthies that he pressed forward to enter
the Gates of Heaven—but in vain. The poem ends, as it
began, with Southey listening to a church bell tolling for the
king's death.

In a controversial preface, Southey attacked what he
called the 'Satanic school' among modern poets. Their
work, he said, was sometimes lascivious, sometimes loath-
some, and was 'more especially characterized by a Satanic
spirit of pride and audacious impiety, which still betrays the
wretched feeling of hopelessness wherewith it is allied'.
The poet whom Southey had chiefly in mind here was
Byron, who retaliated with truly diabolical effectiveness.
The 'Satanic' poet's 'Vision of Judgement' broadly accepts
Southey's account of what happened before the gates of
heaven, but gives it an interpretation much less flattering to
George III and the Laureate. Southey alleged that the Devil
had put up two of the King's chief antagonists to testify
against him—John Wilkes and the mysterious Junius; but
they were ashamed of themselves, and held their tongues:

> Caitiffs, are ye dumb? cried the multifaced Demon in anger.
> Think ye then by shame to shorten the term of your penance?
> Back to your penal dens!... And with horrible grasp gigantic
> Seizing the guilty pair, he swung them aloft, and in vengeance
> Hurl'd them all abroad, far into the sulphurous darkness.

Byron agrees that they refused to testify, but attributes
Wilkes's refusal to his habitual good-nature, and Junius's to
disdain. He also agrees that Southey was snatched up to the
gates of heaven on this occasion—but the snatching was
done by the devil Asmodeus, anxious to have Southey
damned forthwith for scribbling as though he were 'head
clerk to the Fates'.

There undoubtedly was something irresistibly ludicrous about Southey's attempt to be the National Poet. He was not particularly deferential himself to those in authority, and he had too much of a radical past to live down: a fact neatly underlined in 1817 when his youthful poetic drama 'Wat Tyler' made its first appearance (in a pirated edition) before a delighted public. After 1822, moreover, he stood for a point of view which became steadily more remote from political realities. It was a time of accelerating reform. Some of this was acceptable to him: Peel, for example, was drastically cutting down the number of offences punishable by death. But Southey was wholeheartedly against letting Roman Catholics enter the British Parliament—an attitude which could not be maintained in the face of mounting pressure from Ireland. In 1829 'Catholic Emancipation' was accepted by Parliament, and the following year a new government came into power, pledged to a general reform of the House of Commons. It seemed to Southey that the 'state Omnibus' was rolling smoothly 'down an inclined plane, and towards a precipice'. When he was in London in the autumn of 1830, he met the Duke and Duchess of Kent and their young daughter, the future Queen Victoria, who was brought in to tell him that she had read his *Life of Nelson*. The whole family seemed to Southey to be 'as unconcerned about the state of affairs, and passing their days as pleasantly, as Marie Antoinette in her time of coming troubles'.

He was not as disheartened by politics in his later years as some of his gloomy predictions might suggest. He became a friend of Lord Ashley (afterwards Lord Shaftesbury), and saw in him the type of man who would come forward, after the revolution had run its course, to re-edify the Constitution. Southey encouraged him in his interest in factory reform, the more so as most Conservatives in Parliament neglected the issue. ('Verily, verily', said Southey, in a moment of exasperation, 'they seem to be demented.') He warned Ashley, however, against actually visiting the manufacturing districts for fear that his health might suffer from 'the distressful recollections which would be impressed upon you and *burnt in*'. Even now, Southey had evidently not lost his overmastering sensibility.

He himself took no active part in politics. Nothing could tempt him to quit his retreat in Keswick: certainly not the offer he once received to join *The Times* newspaper, nor the seat in Parliament that Lord Radnor wanted him to take in 1826. Apart from his occasional journeys, he spent his life in quiet and constant literary work. He was a model father of his family, a kindly and diplomatic president of a small pantisocratic republic, where no servant was allowed to address the children as Master or Miss. The atmosphere of the place is suggested by a letter which Southey wrote in 1812, when Keswick was alarmed by the presence of 'ugly fellows': unemployed labourers from neighbouring industrial towns. He was asking a friend to send two pistols and a watchman's rattle. The rattle was to give the alarm when the ugly fellows arrived, but Southey looked forward to 'the glorious tunes, the solos and bravuras, that I shall play upon that noble musical instrument before any such fellow makes his appearance'. Southey's son Cuthbert comments gravely that 'these musical anticipations were fully realized'.

Unfortunately the ills of life were not always to be warded off so cheerfully. He was tenderly attached to his eldest son Herbert, and had great hopes of him. But he died in 1816, when only nine years old. Southey was so deeply distressed that his spirits never fully recovered. His wife was even more severely affected by the death ten years later of their daughter Isabel, and eventually lost her reason. After her death (in 1837), Southey married the poet Caroline Bowles, but shortly afterwards his own mind began to fail. He became incapable of recognizing his friends, or of reading. It can be said, however, that he never lost his love of books. He was to be seen in his magnificent library, patting his books affectionately, like a child. He died on 21 March, 1843.

III

Is Southey's poetry still worth reading?

He himself put a high value on his long narrative poems.
They have had their admirers, it is true, including Shelley
and Cardinal Newman, but readers generally have agreed to
ignore them. Richard Porson remarked, with a fine am-
biguity, that ' "Madoc" will be read—when Homer and
Virgil are forgotten'; and, as Byron was careful to explain,
not till then.

If Southey's epics fail to hold the attention, it is because
he so often fails to involve himself deeply enough in the
situations he describes. He lived in a time of appalling
political earthquakes, and the subjects of his poems reflect
this quite explicitly—too explicitly. In such an epoch,
Southey believed, the indispensable virtue was courage, the
willingness to act; and action sometimes depends on shutting
out perceptions that might be disconcerting. More than
once he remarked that 'composition, where any passion is
called forth, excites me more than it is desirable to be
excited'. The writing of poetry could make his face burn
and his heart throb. The real themes of his poetry haunted
the threshold of his consciousness, but seem always to have
been held back, except when disguised in comic forms. He
recorded many of his dreams, and these are sometimes
illuminating. In one dream he was haunted by evil spirits.
He tried to reason himself into a belief in their unreality,
but the horrors continued to increase:

At length an arm appeared through the half-opened door, or rather a
long hand. Determined to convince myself that all was unsubstantial and
visionary, though I saw it most distinctly, I ran up and caught it. It was a
hand, and a lifeless one. I pulled at it with desperate effort, dragged in a
sort of shapeless body into the room, trampled upon it, crying out aloud
the while for horror.

His cries were real enough, and woke up his wife, who in
turn woke him, thus delivering him from the most violent

fear that ever possessed him. He felt, he said, like a mediaeval monk engaged in a contest with the Devil—though one imagines that a devil with horns and tail would have been less frightening than this shapeless horror. Only the annihilation of the feared object would give him a feeling of security, or so it seemed during the dream.

Southey rarely explored the sense of impotence that haunted him in this nightmare, though there is a fine example in his *History of the Peninsular War*. In 1808, Ferdinand of Spain went to Bayonne and thus entered a trap prepared for him by the French:

Confused and terrified as Ferdinand was, and feeling himself in the power of the French, the only ease he could find was by endeavouring implicitly to believe their protestations of friendship.

Southey could hardly have endured this story if he had not known there was to be a happy ending. A power lay dormant in Spain of which the possessors themselves had not suspected the existence until the insurrection broke out. 'The holiest and deepest feelings of the Spanish heart were roused, and the impulse was felt throughout the Peninsula like some convulsion of the earth or elements.'

'The sense of power', Southey said of one of his heroes, 'revived his heart.' Much of his poetry was written to reinforce that sense of power, and his epics glorify the man who never loses his nerve in unpredictable and frightful situations. They are, above all, poems of violence. The domestic pieties, and what he calls 'the healing power of nature', are evident enough, but it is the battle scenes which really engage his poetic energies. This is already clear in his earliest major poem, 'Joan of Arc'. It is best read in the first edition of 1796, where the author's revolutionary sentiments have not been toned down. Not that any revisions could ever do much to soften an English epic which presents the English as wolfish invaders. But later editions somewhat

moderate the 'fierce and terrible benevolence' of the
original:

> To England friendly as to all the world,
> Foe only to the great blood-guilty ones,
> The masters and the murderers of mankind.

The poem is informed with a faith that the oppressed can be
roused to

> Dash down his Moloch-idols, Samson-like,
> And burst his fetters—only strong whilst strong
> Believed.

The climax comes with Joan's address to the newly-crowned
King of France. She bids him rule justly, assuring him that

> hireling guards,
> Tho' flesh'd in slaughter, would be weak to save
> A tyrant on the blood-cemented Throne
> That totters underneath him.

The burning of Joan of Arc, although at one time Southey
thought of writing a play on the subject, is not given any
prominence. Passive suffering was too uncongenial to his
imagination. If an innocent maiden were condemned to be
burnt alive, his natural impulse was to save her by miracle
and blast the perpetrators of the wicked deed: as he contrived
to do in one of his shorter poems, 'The Rose'. But with Joan,
history would not permit this.

In 'Thalaba the Destroyer' (1801) the shackles of history
are cast aside. The hero is an Arabian youth destined to
destroy the evil magicians who live in the Domdaniel
Caverns 'underneath the roots of Ocean'. The magicians try
to destroy Thalaba first, but are always cheated by the
courage and piety inspired by his sense of mission, or by the
direct intervention of providence. Thus, Abdaldar seeks to
stab Thalaba while the latter is prostrate in prayer. The hot
blast of the Simoom passes just at the right moment, and
Abdaldar is suffocated while the pious worshippers

remain unharmed beneath the poisonous whirlwind. At one point Thalaba is taunted with trusting in the magic powers of a ring he took from Abdaldar's corpse. He replies:

> Blindly the wicked work
> The righteous will of Heaven!
> Sayest thou that diffident of God,
> In Magic spells I trust?
> Liar! let witness this!

And he throws the ring into the abyss, where it is caught by a skinny hand. Thus to renounce the aid of magic is no great sacrifice, because high-wrought feeling

> Infused a force portentous, like the strength
> Of madness through his frame

and he is able to throw his antagonist after the ring.

The poem ends with Thalaba's mysteriously-guided journey to the Domdaniel Caves. He travels in a dog-sleigh, and then in a little boat: a part of the poem which delighted the young Shelley, whose 'Alastor' is plainly indebted to it. Thalaba is parachuted down a deep cavern to the roots of Ocean, and there stabs the Giant Idol of the magicians' god, Eblis. The ocean-vault falls in, destroying the magicians along with Thalaba himself, whose soul is immediately translated to paradise.

Cardinal Newman greatly admired the 'irrepressible onward movement' of this poem, leading as it did to a 'tremendous catastrophe in which the hero dying achieves his victory'. What is surprising in this judgement is Newman's feeling that the catastrophe is 'tremendous'. The perils of Thalaba's adventures are so readily overcome that it is difficult to feel much concern about them. For Newman, perhaps, this was one of the poem's merits.

The perils in 'Madoc' (1805) are felt much more intensely. It tells the story of a mediaeval Welsh prince who left the feuds of his native land to settle in America. The first part, 'Madoc in Wales', describes the hero's recruitment of a party of emigrants; the second part, 'Madoc in Aztlan', describes the merciless struggle with the people of Aztlan—ancestors of the Mexicans whom the Spaniards discovered in the sixteenth century. The climax of the poem is the night when Aztec priests and people wait for the sun to rise at the beginning of a new era—wait with a torturing fear that it may never rise again:

> Oppressive, motionless,
> It was a labour and a pain to breathe
> The close, hot, heavy air. Hark! from the woods
> The howl of their wild tenants! and the birds,
> The day-birds, in blind darkness fluttering,
> Fearful to rest, uttering portentous cries!

What follows in fact is a devastating volcanic explosion:

> Anon, the sound of distant thunders came:
> They peal beneath their feet. Earth shakes and yawns,
> And lo! upon the sacred mountain's top,
> The light . . . the mighty flame! A cataract
> Of fire bursts upward from the mountain head, . . .
> High, . . . high, . . . it shoots! the liquid fire boils out;
> It streams in torrents down!

Even though the Aztecs are presented as an exceedingly dangerous enemy, Southey allows his imagination to overwhelm them here with a violence understandable only when one remembers the shapeless horror of his nightmare.

'The Curse of Kehama' (1810) is closer to the manner of 'Thalaba'. The exotic subject, suggested by Southey's reading of Hindu myth and legend, gives considerable scope to his predilection for images of power. Power in this poem is concentrated in the great and wicked figure of Kehama. By the performance of prescribed sacrifices, he has attained semi-divine status, and is attempting to consolidate his conquest of the lower regions of the universe. His son Arvalan had tried to rape Kailyal, a peasant girl, but had been killed in the attempt by her father, Ladurlad. Ladurlad is condemned to the severest torture Kehama can devise: a total deprivation of all satisfactions of the senses. He can never sleep, and must endure an everlasting fire in his heart and brain. To linger out the punishment, Ladurlad is protected by a charm from all possible causes of death. He is thus enabled to thwart Kehama's will, intervening to desecrate the great sacrifice which was to have made Kehama absolute master of hell and earth and the lower heavens. The setback is only temporary, for at the end of the poem Kehama appears to be achieving the final step to omnipotence by drinking the amreeta cup. In fact he is condemning himself to an eternity of torment. Three statues already support the throne of judgement in the underworld: one is the first man who heaped up superfluous wealth, another the first king and conqueror, and another the first deceiving priest. Kehama is transformed into the fourth statue. Ladurlad is then released from the curse, while his daughter joins a beautiful spirit, the Glendoveer, with whom she lives in heaven happy ever after.

Kehama was for Southey a type of the presumptuous will and intellect that threatened old pieties and released infernal energies to devastate the world. In his letters he compares Kehama to Napoleon, and the poem itself makes clear the alliance between Kehama and demonic subversion. In Padalon, the Hindu hell, the rebel spirits lie in chains, but Kehama has filled them with hope. Gigantic demons are constantly having to rivet the rebels' chains to repress their rage:

> Loud around,
> In mingled sound, the echoing lash, the clash
> Of chains, the ponderous hammer's iron stroke,
> With execrations, groans, and shrieks and cries
> Combined in one wild dissonance, arise;
> And through the din there broke,
> Like thunder heard through all the warring winds,
> The dreadful name. Kehama, still they rave,
> Hasten and save!
> Now, now, Deliverer! now, Kehama, now!
> Earthly Almighty, wherefore tarriest thou?

The stoic resistance and domestic piety of Ladurlad and his daughter, the ethereal daring of the Glendoveer, can offer no decisive act of resistance to Kehama. But their firm conviction that 'they who suffer bravely save mankind' enables them to co-operate with the ultimately beneficent purposes of providence. Kehama is defeated in the end only by the mightiest of the gods: Seeva, the Destroyer.

The fifth of Southey's epic poems, 'Roderick, the Last of the Goths', has a wider range of feeling than any of its predecessors. He was more genuinely involved in this Spanish subject than he had been in the others. It tells the story of the Moorish invasion of Spain in the eighth century, and is obviously inspired by Southey's admiration for Spanish and Portuguese resistance to the French during the Peninsular War. It appeared, indeed, in 1814, not long after the end of the fighting. The theme of resistance to misbelievers is combined with others which deeply interested him. Roderick, the last Gothic King of Spain, raped Count Julian's daughter. Count Julian called in the Moors to avenge the wrong, and thus led to the subjection of his country. Roderick, repentant, travelled about Spain in disguise as a priest, helping the forces that were consolidating behind Prince Pelayo, until the first victories against the Moors were achieved. In the battle at the end of the poem, Roderick revealed himself, thus adding to the confusion of the Moors, but afterwards disappeared again.

The poem is exceptional in the extent of the interest that Southey shows in the relationship between Roderick and Count Julian's daughter, Florinda. He is not usually much attracted to love as a subject for poetry, and once remarked that he would like to see the tales which Jean-Pierre Camus, Bishop of Belley, wrote to inspire horror and disgust for the passion. Although Southey does not go so far as the bishop, he certainly tends to relate the passionate forms of love to pain and destruction. If he puts Sappho into one of his early monodramas, she is about to commit suicide. If the beautiful Laila, in 'The Lovers' Rock', runs away with her lover

Manuel from her Moorish home, they are trapped on the way and throw themselves down a precipice rather than risk dying separately. In three major poems, 'Wat Tyler', 'The Curse of Kehama', and 'Roderick', rape or attempted rape forms a conspicuous part of the plot. In 'Roderick', however, the guilty man is a sympathetic character. We come to see that the rape is hardly a rape at all: Florinda was in love with Roderick, and she resisted him on account of a rash vow she had made to live as a hermit.

As in all the other epics, however, it is the violence which impresses itself most memorably. The experience which Southey finds unendurable is the sense of 'joyless, helpless, hopeless servitude', not only to the Moors, but to the very nature of things. In fighting the Moors, the Spaniards are comforted and reconciled to life, above all at a moment like the Battle of Covadanga, when the Moorish army is lured into a deep valley, and then crushed by a landslide set in motion by Pelayo's force:

> The Asturians shouting in the name of God,
> Set the whole ruin loose! huge trunks and stones,
> And loosen'd crags, down, down they roll'd with rush
> And bound, and thundering force.

The poem reaches its climax in the battle where Roderick throws off his disguise, rejoicing in his strength. He lays about him with his good sword,

> and smote
> And overthrew, and scatter'd, and destroy'd,
> And trampled down.

Much as Southey might enjoy celebrating battles in poetry, he did not care for the real thing. In the late summer of 1815, he visited the field of the Battle of Waterloo. He was much distressed by the condition of the soldiers who were recovering from their wounds, and remarked that he had never before seen the real face of war so closely:

'God knows!' he added, 'a deplorable sight it is.' His laureate poem on the subject, 'The Poet's Pilgrimage to Waterloo', is a resolute attempt to digest this melancholy experience. After an account of his visit, he dreamed that he met a tempter who argued that life was sickening and meaningless, undirected by any purpose:

> The winds which have in viewless heaven their birth,
>   The waves which in their fury meet the clouds,
> The central storms which shake the solid earth,
>   And from volcanoes burst in fiery floods,
> Are not more vague and purportless and blind,
> Than is the course of things among mankind!

Southey recovers his optimism when the Heavenly Muse reassures him that human progress is real, and that Britain's civilizing mission in the world will make a great contribution to it. The earlier doubts are suppressed by a firm effort of the will, however, rather than through any deeply-felt assurance.

The most pleasing of his longer poems is also the most unreservedly sombre. This is 'A Tale of Paraguay', which was published in 1825. It tells of a small family who were the only survivors of a smallpox epidemic in a tribe of Guarini Indians. Mother, son, and daughter were eventually brought into one of the Jesuit settlements, where, although kindly treated, they soon died. The poem is Southey's most extensive and deliberate account of the insecurity to which human life is exposed. Disease, war, predatory animals—all help to make men's hold on life a frail one. Settlement in the Jesuit 'reduction' appears to remove the most apparent causes of insecurity, but in fact the change in the way of life of 'these poor children of the solitude' proves more deadly than anything else. Dobrizhoffer, the Austrian Jesuit who ruled the reduction, was deeply grieved when first the mother, then the daughter died: but neither of them felt distress. The daughter saw him weep,

> and she could understand
> The cause thus tremulously that made him speak.
> By his emotion mov'd she took his hand;
> A gleam of pleasure o'er her pallid cheek
> Pass'd, while she look'd at him with meaning meek,
> And for a little while, as loth to part,
> Detaining him, her fingers lank and weak,
> Play'd with their hold; then letting him depart
> She gave him a slow smile that touch'd him to the heart.

Something is expressed here of Southey's own most painful experiences—the deaths of his children. It was made bearable for him by the remoteness of the subject, and by the feeling that it was better for these Indians to die under Dobrizhoffer's benevolent care than to survive his expulsion along with the other Jesuits in 1767, when 'all of good that Paraguay enjoy'd' was overthrown 'by blind and suicidal Power'.

Impressive in its own way as 'A Tale of Paraguay' is, however, it is not resilient enough to be fully characteristic of Southey. His buoyancy finds its most natural expression in many of his shorter poems, especially those in which the Devil plays a part. There is St. Romuald, for example, who used to fight with Satan 'all through a winter's night' until

> his face became
> All black and yellow with the brimstone flame,
> And then he smelt—O Lord! how he did smell!

While Southey usually contrives to keep the Devil at bay, some of his most memorable ballads re-enact the nightmare of being overpowered by an alien will. This experience could be made palatable by attributing great wickedness to the victim, as in 'God's Judgement on a Wicked Bishop'. It is mere poetic justice to be eaten by thousands of rats when you have just burned a barn crowded with women and children. 'The Old Woman of Berkeley' is a little more disquieting. It tells how a witch was carried off by the Devil in spite of the devoted efforts of a large company of priests, choristers, and bellmen, and the protection of a stone coffin fastened by iron bars and tied down by three chains, blessed and sprinkled with holy water. The Old Woman may be a witch, but one cannot help feeling for her—or at least for the priest her son and the nun her daughter, who labour so diligently for their mother's salvation, and to no effect. This ballad is said to have been translated into Russian, and its publication prohibited, because children were frightened by it.

By contrast, the Russian authorities would have found a poem that Southey wrote some thirty years later positively edifying. This was 'The Young Dragon'. It was founded on a Spanish legend about Antioch in early Christian days. Satan was alarmed at the number of conversions to Christianity there, and hatched out a dragon to punish the city. This dragon required a Christian virgin every day, and when a certain Marana was chosen, her father (a pagan) took active measures to save her life. He stole the thumb of John the Baptist, preserved as a relic in Antioch, and just as the dragon was about to devour his daughter, lobbed it down the dragon's throat. The effect was remarkable:

> A rumbling and a tumbling
>   Was heard in his inside,
> He gasp'd, he panted, he lay down,
>   He roll'd from side to side:
> He moan'd, he groan'd, he snuff'd, he snor'd,
> He growl'd, he howl'd, he rav'd, he roar'd;
>   But loud as were his clamours,
> Far louder was the inward din,
> Like a hundred braziers working in
>   A caldron with their hammers.

His body swelled up, rose slowly from the ground, and, when three miles up, exploded with a sound that could be heard a hundred leagues away. The débris was dispersed like the fall-out from a nuclear explosion, and the Holy Thumb ascended to heaven.

Southey's best work is often his most playful, as is shown by 'The Story of the Three Bears'.[1] It is a beautifully poised treatment of the theme of the unamiable protagonist whose sins get her into trouble. (The amiable Goldilocks belongs to a decadent version.) The impudent old woman, who eats the little bear's porridge, pushes the bottom out of his chair, and goes to sleep in his bed, is surely well-advised to jump out of the window when the bears discover her. But nothing worse happens than complaints from the Great Huge Bear in his great rough, gruff voice—represented by 𝕲𝖗𝖊𝖆𝖙 𝕳𝖚𝖌𝖊 𝕲𝖔𝖙𝖍𝖎𝖈 𝕿𝖞𝖕𝖊.

The story belongs to a world which Southey did not generally believe in: a golden world where bears do nobody any harm, and never suspect that anybody will harm them. A more characteristic view of life is suggested in that famous early poem 'The Battle of Blenheim'. Here he is content to juxtapose the world of domestic decency with the dreadful world of power. It reflects both sides of his character: his inborn kindliness and sensitivity, and his unwilling conviction that the world is a savage place. Old Kaspar, talking to Peterkin and Wilhelmine about the many thousand bodies that 'lay rotting in the sun', makes Southey's point with a fine economy:

> 'Great praise the Duke of Marlbro' won
>   And our good Prince Eugene.'
> 'Why 'twas a very wicked thing!'
>   Said little Wilhelmine.
> 'Nay—nay—my little girl', quoth he,
> 'It was a famous victory.'

IV

Southey's prose is vigorous, direct, and covers much ground in little time. 'My way', he said once, 'is when I see

[1]First published in Vol. IV of his desultory novel *The Doctor*, in 1837.

my object, to dart at it like a greyhound.' Unfortunately he
often pays for this vigour by oversimplifying the issues. He
is too anxious to reach an assured position to have time to
unravel complexities. He does not suppress the contra-
dictory feelings that influence his views, but they appear as
fluctuations of opinion and feeling, not as constituents of a
consistent attitude. When he was considering Roman
Catholicism in the context of current British politics, he used
language of unqualified hostility:

Wherever the Roman Catholic superstition predominates, it offers only
these alternatives:— Unbelief, with scarce a decent covering of hypo-
crisy, and all the abominations of vice, as exhibited in Italy and France,
among the higher ranks; or base, abject, degrading destructive bigotry
in all, as in Spain, Portugal, and the Austrian States. These are the
effects which always have been, and always must be, produced by a
Catholic establishment.

Edinburgh Annual Register for 1808.

Southey wrote these words while he was working on
'Roderick', a poem which might have come from the pen
of a Catholic apologist. 'A Tale of Paraguay' and the
History of Brazil show how warmly he felt towards the
Jesuits of South America. It might be possible to reconcile
the various opinions that Southey expresses so vehemently;
but Southey himself did not make any very adequate
attempt.

The same is true of his attitude towards the protestant sect
of the Quakers. He was united with them in steadfast
opposition to slavery, in their warm but undogmatic
religious feeling, in their stoic discipline of life, and their
practical goodwill. He once expressed a wish that he could
bring up his son Herbert as a Quaker. In some moods he
could feel that pacifism was a practical policy. He believed
that the Quakers of Pennsylvania had shown that 'a people
whose principle it is never to resist evil, and always to bear
testimony against it, cannot be crushed by any exertion of
human power short of universal massacre'. At one time he

supported the abolition of all capital punishment, on the ground that this example would produce a more general reverence for life. He also proposed that the management of British prisons should be entirely handed over to the Quakers. But even at the time of his greatest sympathy with Quakerism, around 1807, he was apt to express warlike and unquakerly views. Quakerism, he told someone, is the true system of the Gospel, 'but I want to have the invasion over before I allow it to be so'.

His attitude towards John Wesley and the Methodist movement was more consistent, and his *Life of Wesley* is in many ways a valuable contribution to the religious history of Britain in the eighteenth century. Southey was well versed in Methodist literature, and reduces a mass of documentation to a clear and workmanlike narrative. But he is not fully in sympathy with his subject. His imagination could be deeply stirred by Catholicism; he could contemplate bringing up his best-loved son as a Quaker. He felt no such involvement with this predominantly working-class religious movement. Originally fiercely hostile to it, he gradually developed an attitude of measured respect. He recognized that Wesley had reclaimed many from a course of sin, supported many in poverty, sickness, and affliction, and imparted to many a triumphant joy in death. But one continually feels that Southey has a certain distaste for the Methodists, and the book leaves one with a sense of having surveyed Methodism from the outside, not with having gained much understanding of the inner dynamics of the movement.

In his *Letters from England*, however, this kind of detachment is turned to good account. It was published (in 1807) as the work of a Spanish traveller, Don Manuel Alvarez Espriella, and Southey enters spiritedly into the part of a Catholic and a foreigner. He speaks of fashions in dress, furniture, and religion, of quackery and dishonesty of many kinds. He is deeply impressed by 'the ingenuity, the activity, and the indefatigable watchfulness of roguery in England'.

He visits the picturesque Lake District, and tells of the cheap
boarding schools in Yorkshire—later to be pilloried by
Dickens in *Nicholas Nickleby*. There is an eloquent account
of the evils of life in industrial Manchester. He is interested in
crowd behaviour, and gives several striking examples of it.
He goes into great detail about the religious underworld,
seeing here evidence of a deep social current flowing he
knows not where. Southey is obviously fascinated by
incidents like Joanna Southcott's debate with the Devil:
it is a subject he might have used in a ballad. The book lives
because of its vivid presentation of the surface of life in early
nineteenth-century England; but it is a surface which
invites the reader to speculate, with Don Manuel, about
what is going on below.

His critique of industrial society is more fully developed
in a series of imaginary conversations between himself and
the ghost of Sir Thomas More which he published in 1829:
the *Colloquies on the Progress and Prospects of Society*. In spite
of More's Catholicism, Southey felt deeply in sympathy
with him. Had he not conceived the original Utopia? And
might not Southey himself have resisted the protestant
reformation if he had been a contemporary of More's? 'I
resisted opinions', he makes More say, 'which in their sure
consequences led to anarchy in all things.' Southey's own
revulsion against anarchy led him to endorse the co-
operative projects of Robert Owen, and to revive the idea of
a protestant order of Sisters of Charity. His book is a notable
monument of the nineteenth-century rebellion against 'the
devouring principle of trade'.

None of Southey's other prose works, however, has quite
the vitality of the *Life of Nelson*. There was a real sympathy
of spirit between the poet and the admiral. Southey saw in
this man who could not bear tame or slow measures a
superb example of the leadership needed in such portentous
times as his. Vexed and disappointed as he might sometimes
unavoidably be, Nelson had the resilient spirit that Southey
valued in himself. Nelson, he said, had 'that lively spring of

hope within him, which partakes enough of the nature of faith to work miracles in war'. Once he was engaged in action, 'his conversation became joyous, animated, elevated, and delightful'. Even in his death agonies during the Battle of Trafalgar, the same spirit persisted. When the surgeon asked him whether his pain was very great, 'he replied, "So great, that he wished he was dead. Yet", said he, in a lower voice, "one would like to live a little longer too!" ' The affinity to Thalaba and Roderick is evident: but Southey's Nelson is a finer creation than his other heroes. None of them combines so convincingly the qualities of courage and kindliness:

He governed men by their reason and their affections: they knew that he was incapable of caprice or tyranny; and they obeyed him with alacrity and joy, because he possessed their confidence as well as their love. 'Our Nel', they used to say, 'is as brave as a lion, and as gentle as a lamb.' Severe discipline he detested, though he had been bred in a severe school: he never inflicted corporal punishment if it were possible to avoid it and when compelled to enforce it, he, who was familiar with wounds and death, suffered like a woman.

On his own initiative, Southey would not have made one of his heroes irritable through 'fatigue, and anxiety, and vexation at the dilatory measures of the commander-in-chief'. Not that such irritation was outside his experience. On the contrary, Southey the *Quarterly* reviewer was constantly complaining that his most effective blows were spoiled by the cowardly editor. Nelson among the Neapolitans plainly looked, in Southey's eyes, just like himself among the politicians who controlled the *Quarterly Review*. Nelson, he said,

saw selfishness and knavery wherever he looked; and even the pleasure of seeing the cause prosper, in which he was so zealously engaged, was poisoned by his sense of the rascality of those with whom he was compelled to act.

But Southey did not write poetry about such complexities.

He has been much criticized for his censorious comments on Nelson's attachment to Lady Hamilton. It is true that irregular love-affairs were as uncongenial to Southey as the finer points of tactics, but he admired Lady Hamilton in her rôle as encourager of heroism, and acknowledges her 'uncommon intellectual endowments'. Her worst sin, from Southey's point of view, was undue devotion to the Neapolitan court. He thought this was about the worst government that had ever existed. If the revolutionary spirit of the 1790's had been allowed to sweep away such rotten régimes—if Britain had not interfered in their favour—Southey would have been well pleased. When Lady Hamilton appeared to him to act as the agent of such a government, no words of condemnation could be too strong. It must be admitted, however, that Southey's considered opinion of Lady Hamilton is as difficult to assess as his considered opinion of the Roman Catholic Church.

V

Southey himself is not much easier to sum up. There can be no doubt of his kindness, his willingness to help, and the utter reliability that made such help really useful. But there is an unmistakable element of hardness in his character. He could be a severe judge of other people, especially if political issues were involved. Once outside the security of his domestic life, he felt himself to be in a world where ruthlessness was necessary to survival. He was always at the mercy of his emotions. Even in his sixties he would still blush with pleasure like a girl, or turn slate-coloured with anger. 'How has he not been torn to pieces long since', Thomas Carlyle asked himself, 'under such furious pulling this way and that?' He could be extraordinarily timid, too— at least in unfamiliar situations. In 1834 John Lingard summoned Wordsworth and Southey to give evidence on a literary point in a lawsuit. Wordsworth spoke boldly, looking the very figure of a robust mountaineer, 'his shirt unbuttoned in the front, disclosing a tough and hairy breast'. But there was nothing so robust about Southey. He could be brought to say no more than that he agreed with Wordsworth's testimony.

Southey often contemplated the idea of emigrating, thinking not only of North America, but at various times of Switzerland, Portugal, Brazil, and Australia. A similar impulse prompted his enthusiasm for projects of large-scale emigration for the working classes, as well as for the transportation of seditious journalists and politicians. Anything that relieved the menacing pressure of life in industrial England was welcome. The appeal of emigration was purely ideal, of course, so far as he himself was concerned. Keswick served well enough as a retreat, and his library of 14,000 volumes was a secure vantage-point for viewing the problems of man and society—as he did in his *Colloquies* with the ghost of Sir Thomas More. Southey's poems and histories are inspired by current events and feelings, but the source-materials (cited in notes which often crowd out the text) interpose a thick screen between the world and his sensibility:

> My days among the Dead are pass'd;
>   Around me I behold,
> Where'er these casual eyes are cast,
>   The mighty minds of old . . .

The 'casual' is significant. Here at least Southey could afford to take his ease. Downstairs young Herbert might be playing at Apollyon in the *Pilgrim's Progress*, roaring at his sisters like a lion seeking whom he might devour: but that was as near as the Devil, and the alarming energies that he symbolized, ever got to Greta Hall. Except in dreams.

ROBERT SOUTHEY

A Select Bibliography

(Place of publication London, unless stated otherwise)

Bibliography:

THE EARLY LIFE OF ROBERT SOUTHEY, by William Haller. New York (1917)

—Appendix A is a detailed descriptive list of Southey's works, but does not include contributions to periodicals.

THE ENGLISH ROMANTIC POETS AND ESSAYISTS: A REVIEW OF RESEARCH AND CRITICISM. ed. C. W. Houtchens and L. H. Houtchens. Modern Language Association of America, New York (1957)

—the chapter on Southey, by Kenneth Curry, is the fullest bibliographical guide available.

Collected Works:

THE POETICAL WORKS OF ROBERT SOUTHEY, COLLECTED BY HIMSELF. 10 vols. (1837-38)

—reprinted several times in one volume.

POEMS OF ROBERT SOUTHEY, ed. M. H. Fitzgerald (1909)

—contains bibliographical notes, but omits 'Joan of Arc', 'A Vision of Judgement', and some minor poems.

SELECT PROSE OF ROBERT SOUTHEY, ed. Jacob Zeitlin. New York (1916)

—selected passages only.

Separate Works:

THE FALL OF ROBESPIERRE: AN HISTORIC DRAMA, by S. T. Coleridge. Cambridge (1794). *Verse*

—Coleridge wrote Act I, Southey Acts II and III.

POEMS: . . . BY ROBERT LOVELL, AND ROBERT SOUTHEY. Bath (1795).

JOAN OF ARC, AN EPIC POEM. Bristol (1796)

—revised editions in 1798, 1806 and 1812. Some further revisions were made in the *Poetical Works* of 1837-38.

POEMS, BY ROBERT SOUTHEY. Bristol (1797)

—a second, revised, edition appeared in 1797, and a second volume in 1799.

LETTERS WRITTEN DURING A SHORT RESIDENCE IN SPAIN AND PORTUGAL. Bristol (1797).

THALABA THE DESTROYER. 2 vols. (1801). *Verse*

MADOC (1805). *Verse*

METRICAL TALES AND OTHER POEMS (1805).

LETTERS FROM ENGLAND: BY DON MANUEL ALVAREZ ESPRIELLA. 3 vols.
(1807)

—there is a modern reprint, edited by Jack Simmons (1951).

THE CURSE OF KEHAMA (1810). *Verse*

HISTORY OF BRAZIL. Vol. 1 (1810)

—vol. 2 appeared in 1817, vol. 3 in 1819.

OMNIANA, OR HORAE OTIOSIORES. 2 vols. (1812)

—by Southey and Coleridge.

THE ORIGIN, NATURE, AND OBJECT OF THE NEW SYSTEM OF EDUCATION
(1812).

THE LIFE OF NELSON. 2 vols. (1813)

—revised editions in 1814 and 1830. The best modern edition is by
Geoffrey Callender (1922). The text of the first edition is available
in Everyman's Library and Nelson Classics.

RODERICK, THE LAST OF THE GOTHS (1814). *Verse*

ODES TO HIS ROYAL HIGHNESS THE PRINCE REGENT, HIS IMPERIAL MAJESTY
THE EMPEROR OF RUSSIA, AND HIS MAJESTY THE KING OF PRUSSIA (1814).

CARMEN TRIUMPHALE, FOR THE COMMENCEMENT OF THE YEAR 1814 (1814).

THE MINOR POEMS OF ROBERT SOUTHEY. 3 vols. (1815)

—reprints *Poems* and *Metrical Tales*.

THE POET'S PILGRIMAGE TO WATERLOO (1816). *Verse*

THE LAY OF THE LAUREATE. CARMEN NUPTIALE (1816).

WAT TYLER (1817). *Verse*

A LETTER TO WILLIAM SMITH, ESQ., M.P. (1817).

THE LIFE OF WESLEY; AND THE RISE AND PROGRESS OF METHODISM.
2 vols. (1820)

—there is a modern reprint, edited by M. H. Fitzgerald (1925).

A VISION OF JUDGEMENT (1821). *Verse*

THE EXPEDITION OF ORSUA; AND THE CRIMES OF AGUIRRE (1821).

HISTORY OF THE PENINSULAR WAR. Vol. 1 (1823)

—vol. 2 appeared in 1827, vol. 3 in 1832.

THE BOOK OF THE CHURCH (1824).

A TALE OF PARAGUAY (1825). *Verse*

VINDICIAE ECCLESIAE ANGLICANAE. LETTERS TO CHARLES BUTLER, ESQ.,
COMPRISING ESSAYS ON THE ROMISH RELIGION AND VINDICATING THE
BOOK OF THE CHURCH (1826).

ALL FOR LOVE; AND THE PILGRIM TO COMPOSTELLA (1829). *Verse*

SIR THOMAS MORE: OR, COLLOQUIES ON THE PROGRESS AND PROSPECTS OF SOCIETY. 2 vols. (1829).

ESSAYS, MORAL AND POLITICAL. 2 vols. (1832).

LIVES OF THE BRITISH ADMIRALS. vols. 1 and 2 (1833)

—vol. 3 appeared in 1834, vol. 4 in 1837. Reprinted as *English Seamen*, edited by David Hannay (1895).

LETTER TO JOHN MURRAY, ESQ., 'TOUCHING' LORD NUGENT (1833).

THE DOCTOR. Vols. 1 and 2 (1834)

—vol. 3 appeared in 1835, vol. 4 in 1837, vol. 5 in 1838, and vols. 6 and 7 in 1847. There is a modern (abridged) edition by M. H. Fitzgerald (1930).

THE LIFE OF THE REV. ANDREW BELL. 3 vols. (1844)

—vol. 1 by Southey, vols. 2 and 3 by his son C. C. Southey.

OLIVER NEWMAN: A NEW-ENGLAND TALE (UNFINISHED): WITH OTHER POETICAL REMAINS (1845).

ROBIN HOOD: A FRAGMENT. BY THE LATE ROBERT SOUTHEY, AND CAROLINE SOUTHEY (1847). *Verse.*

SOUTHEY'S COMMON-PLACE BOOK, ed. J. W. Warter. 4 vols. (1849-51).

JOURNAL OF A TOUR IN THE NETHERLANDS IN THE AUTUMN OF 1815, ed. W. Robertson Nicoll (1903).

JOURNAL OF A TOUR IN SCOTLAND IN 1819, ed. C. H. Herford (1929).

JOURNALS OF A RESIDENCE IN PORTUGAL, 1800-1801 AND A VISIT TO FRANCE, 1838, ed. Adolfo Cabral. Oxford (1960).

See also the following section for Southey's biographies of Kirke White, John Bunyan, Isaac Watts, and William Cowper.

Works Edited or Translated by Southey:

ON THE FRENCH REVOLUTION, BY MR. NECKER. 2 vols. (1797)
—vol. 2 translated from the French by Southey.

THE WORKS OF THOMAS CHATTERTON. 3 vols. (1803)
—edited by Southey and Joseph Cottle.

AMADIS OF GAUL, BY VASCO LOBEIRA. 4 vols. (1803)
—translated from the Spanish.

THE REMAINS OF HENRY KIRKE WHITE. 2 vols. (1807)
—includes a short biography by Southey. Vol. 3 appeared in 1822.

PALMERIN OF ENGLAND, BY FRANCISCO DE MORAES. 4 vols. (1807)
—translated from the Portuguese.

SPECIMENS OF THE LATER ENGLISH POETS. 3 vols. (1807).

CHRONICLE OF THE CID. (1808)
—translated from the Spanish.

THE BYRTH, LYF, AND ACTES OF KING ARTHUR. 2 vols. (1817).

THE PILGRIM'S PROGRESS. WITH A LIFE OF JOHN BUNYAN (1830).

ATTEMPTS IN VERSE, BY JOHN JONES, AN OLD SERVANT: WITH . . . AN INTRODUCTORY ESSAY ON THE LIVES AND WORKS OF OUR UNEDUCATED POETS (1831)

—the *Essay* was reprinted in 1925, edited by J. S. Childers.

SELECT WORKS OF THE BRITISH POETS, FROM CHAUCER TO JONSON, WITH BIOGRAPHICAL SKETCHES (1831).

HORAE LYRICAE. POEMS . . . BY ISAAC WATTS . . . WITH A MEMOIR OF THE AUTHOR (1834).

THE WORKS OF WILLIAM COWPER. . . . WITH A LIFE OF THE AUTHOR. 15 vols. (1835-37).

Contributions to Periodicals:

Number 5 of the *Flagellant*, 1792, contained Southey's attack on flogging.

Contributions from Southey appeared in the *Monthly Magazine*, 1796-1800; the *Morning Post* (poems), 1798-9; the *Critical Review*, 1798-1803; the *Annual Anthology* (edited by Southey), Bristol, 1799-1800; the *Annual Review*, 1802-8; the *Athenaeum*, 1807-9; the *Edinburgh Annual Register*, Edinburgh, 1808-11, to which Southey contributed the 'History of Europe'; and the *Foreign Review*, 1828-30. For his contributions to the *Quarterly Review*, 1809-39, see *The Quarterly Review under Gifford*, by H. Shine and H. C. Shine. Chapel Hill (1949); and *Life and Correspondence of Robert Southey*, by C. C. Southey, vol. 6 (1850), pp. 400-2 (incomplete). Southey also contributed poems to Annuals like the *Literary Souvenir*, 1826-8, the *Amulet*, 1829, the *Anniversary*, 1829, and the *Keepsake*, 1829.

Letters:

MEMOIR OF THE LIFE AND WRITINGS OF THE LATE WILLIAM TAYLOR, by J. W. Robberds. 2 vols. (1843).

THE LIFE AND CORRESPONDENCE OF ROBERT SOUTHEY, by C. C. Southey. 6 vols. (1849-50).

SELECTIONS FROM THE LETTERS OF ROBERT SOUTHEY, ed. J. W. Warter. 4 vols. (1856).

WALTER SAVAGE LANDOR: A BIOGRAPHY, by J. Forster. 2 vols. (1869).

THE CORRESPONDENCE OF ROBERT SOUTHEY WITH CAROLINE BOWLES, ed. E. Dowden. Dublin (1881).

LAMB'S FRIEND THE CENSUS-TAKER: LIFE AND LETTERS OF JOHN RICKMAN, by O. Williams (1911).

NEW LETTERS OF ROBERT SOUTHEY, ed. K. Curry. 2 vols. New York (1964).

Some Biographical and Critical Studies:

Review of 'Thalaba the Destroyer', by F. Jeffrey, *Edinburgh Review*, 1802

—reprinted in *Famous Reviews*, edited by R. Brimley Johnson (1914).

Review of 'The Curse of Kehama', by John Foster, *Eclectic Review*, 1811

—reprinted in Foster's *Contributions to the Eclectic Review*, vol. 2 (1844). An evangelical-Christian critique.

THE VISION OF JUDGEMENT, by Lord Byron (1822).

THE SPIRIT OF THE AGE, by W. Hazlitt (1825).

Review of *Colloquies of Society*, by T. B. Macaulay, *Edinburgh Review*, 1830

—reprinted in Macaulay's *Critical and Historical Essays*, vol. 1 (1843).

EARLY RECOLLECTIONS, by J. Cottle. 2 vols. (1837)

—revised as *Reminiscences of Samuel Taylor Coleridge and Robert Southey* (1848).

'Lake Reminiscences, from 1807 to 1830. No. IV—William Wordsworth and Robert Southey', by T. De Quincey, *Tait's Edinburgh Magazine*, 1839

—reprinted in De Quincey's *Works*, edited by David Masson, vol. 2. Edinburgh (1889). Also in *Recollections of the Lake Poets*, edited by E. Sackville-West (1948).

SOUTHEY, by E. Dowden (1879).

REMINISCENCES, by T. Carlyle, vol. 2 (1881).

ESSAYS IN ENGLISH LITERATURE, series 2, by G. Saintsbury (1895)

—the essay on Southey is reprinted in Saintsbury's *Collected Essays and Papers*, vol. 1 (1923).

STUDIES OF A BIOGRAPHER, by L. Stephen, vol. 4 (1902).

LECTURES ON THE RELATION BETWEEN LAW AND PUBLIC OPINION IN ENGLAND DURING THE NINETEENTH CENTURY, by A. V. Dicey (1905)

—lecture 7 briefly relates Southey to 'Tory philanthropy'.

THE ROMANTIC MOVEMENT IN ENGLISH POETRY, by A. Symons (1909)

—'Southey had a small but genuine talent of a homely and grotesque order.'

'Robert Southey und Spanien', von L. Pfandl, *Revue hispanique* (1913)
—an exhaustive study.

THE EARLY LIFE OF ROBERT SOUTHEY, by W. Haller. New York (1917)
—the fullest study of Southey as poet.

A HISTORY OF BRITISH SOCIALISM, by M. Beer, vol. 1 (1919)
—Southey as critic of capitalism.

THE LAUREATESHIP. A STUDY OF THE OFFICE OF POET LAUREATE IN
ENGLAND, by E. K. Broadus. Oxford (1921).

POLITICAL IDEAS OF THE ENGLISH ROMANTICISTS, by Crane Brinton (1926)
—Chapter 2.

LA LITTÉRATURE PORTUGAISE EN ANGLETERRE A L'ÉPOQUE ROMANTIQUE,
par F. Walter. Paris (1927)
—Chapter 3.

THE NOBLE SAVAGE, by H. N. Fairchild. New York (1928)
—Chapter 6.

EDMUND BURKE AND THE REVOLT AGAINST THE EIGHTEENTH CENTURY,
by A. Cobban (1929)
—Southey's political and social thinking related to that of Burke,
Wordsworth, and Coleridge.

'Southey's Relations with Finland and Scandinavia', by H. G. Wright,
Modern Language Review, 1932.

THE TRANSITION IN ENGLISH HISTORICAL WRITING, 1760-1830, by
T. P. Peardon. New York (1933)
—Southey's place in the development of historiography.

'Southey and Brazil', by J. de Sousa Leão, *Modern Language Review*,
1943.

SOUTHEY, by J. Simmons (1945)
—the standard biography.

HUMAN DIGNITY AND THE GREAT VICTORIANS, by B. N. Schilling
New York (1946)
—chapter 4. Southey as opponent of orthodox political economy.

THE FIRST ROMANTICS, by M. Elwin (1947)
—biographical account of Wordsworth, Coleridge, and Southey.

GUIDE THROUGH THE ROMANTIC MOVEMENT, by E. Bernbaum. Second
edition. New York (1949)
—excellent brief study and bibliography.

THE POETS LAUREATE, by K. Hopkins (1954).

THE SILENT REBELLION: ANGLICAN RELIGIOUS COMMUNITIES 1845-1900,
by A. M. Allchin (1958)
—emphasizes Southey's contribution to the revival of the idea of
Sisters of Charity.

CULTURE AND SOCIETY 1780-1950, by R. Williams (1958)
—brief discussion of Southey's critique of modern industrial society.

SOUTHEY E PORTUGAL 1774-1801, by A. Cabral. Lisbon (1959)

ROBERT SOUTHEY AND HIS AGE: THE DEVELOPMENT OF A CONSERVATIVE
MIND, by G. Carnall. Oxford (1960).

THE ENCHANTED FOREST, by W. W. Beyer. Oxford (1963)
—Appendix V: 'Southey, Orientalism, and *Thalaba*.'